CONTENTS

T0282098

Chapter 1

Noticing a Difference

When I was younger, I always did well at school. I aced tests and turned in worksheets on time. But now that I'm in ninth grade, I've struggled more. It's harder to stay organized. I forget homework all the time. Sitting still in class is a problem.

My school **counselor** called a meeting with my parents. They were concerned about my falling grades. I felt really scared. What was wrong with me?

They decided to have me tested for learning disabilities. A psychiatrist—a kind of doctor who works with the mind, or mental health—said I have ADHD. I'm so embarrassed. What will my friends say?

ADHD symptoms, or signs, can get worse in high school. This is likely due to an increasing workload. This can make things seem even more difficult, or trying.

DEFINING ADHD

ADHD is a type of mental health condition that changes how a person acts or **behaves**. It stands for attention-deficit/hyperactivity disorder. ADHD is one of the most common mental conditions that affect children. However, many people aren't diagnosed, or told they have the disorder by a doctor, until they're teenagers or adults.

ADHD can look different for different people. Many people have trouble focusing, or paying attention. They may also be hyperactive and struggle at school or work. However, there are many ways to help people with ADHD be successful!

Nearly one in ten U.S. children and teens between the ages of two to 17 have been diagnosed with ADHD.

What's in a Name?

Attention: The ability to focus on something.

Deficit: Lacking.

Attention-Deficit: Lacking the ability to focus.

Hyperactivity: Very active.

Disorder: Health condition.

Hyperactivity Disorder: Active to the point of having a lot of trouble at work or school.

CHANGING TERMS

ADHD used to be known as ADD—attention-deficit disorder. Some people still call it that. In 1987, the American **Psychiatric Association** renamed it ADHD. This put a new focus on the condition of hyperactivity.

SIGNS AND SYMPTOMS

ADHD has many symptoms, or signs. Some can be seen, some can't. Not all people with ADHD have the same symptoms. ADHD symptoms also often change as people get older. Symptoms can be **behavioral**, or they can be **physical**. Here are a few common ADHD symptoms across age groups.

People with ADHD may have trouble staying organized and completing tasks such as homework on time.

Behavioral signs of ADHD:

- Having trouble getting along with people
- Acting impulsively, or hastily
- Daydreaming a lot
- Forgetting or losing things

Physical signs of ADHD:

- Squirming or moving around a lot
- Talking a lot
- Running and climbing at improper times

TYPES OF ADHD

Doctors have broken ADHD into three types because the symptoms can be different. Some people have predominantly, or mostly, inattentive presentation. Others have a mostly hyperactive-impulsive presentation. Some have both. This is called combined (or mixed) presentation.

Symptoms of hyperactivity often lessen as children grow older.

Doctors diagnose people with a certain type of ADHD by looking at their symptoms. Doctors may also diagnose people with "mild," "moderate," or "**severe**" cases of ADHD. A person with ADHD will receive different **treatments** based on their type, severity, age, and past treatments.

Predominantly Inattentive Presentation

People are more likely to have trouble paying attention, following directions, and staying organized. They don't like tasks that need a lot of mental effort, and they lose things.

Predominantly Hyperactive-Impulsive Presentation

People have a hard time sitting still and keeping quiet. They might talk a lot and fidget, which means making small movements with the hands or feet.

ADHD THROUGH HISTORY

Doctors started using the term "ADHD" in the 1980s. The condition, however, has been around much longer. The earliest record of ADHD symptoms happened in ancient Greece. Hippocrates—who lived from about 460 to 375 BCE—wrote about people who couldn't focus for long. He said these people also reacted strongly towards things around them.

In 1902, Sir George Frederic Still was the first to give talks about what is today called ADHD. The British doctor also wrote about it in a popular book of the time.

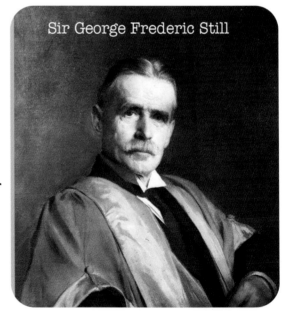
Sir George Frederic Still

The Hippocratic Oath—a set of rules doctors use—is named after Hippocrates. He may or may not have written the oath.

WHO WAS HIPPOCRATES?

Hippocrates is known as the father of medicine. He wrote a lot of important records about medicine. Some people think these writings may not all be by Hippocrates. Knowing little about ADHD then, Hippocrates blamed it on an "overbalance of fire over water."

Also Known As

Throughout history, the condition now known to be ADHD has gone by different names. Many are considered incorrect and rude today.

- Nervous child
- Unstable nervous system
- Mental instability
- ADD

ANYONE CAN HAVE ADHD

Many famous people have been diagnosed with ADHD. Olympic gymnast Simone Biles announced her ADHD diagnosis in 2016. "Having ADHD and taking medicine for it is nothing to be **ashamed** of," she Tweeted. It's "nothing that I'm afraid to let people know."

Gymnast Simone Biles revealed her diagnosis after someone leaked her personal information, or facts.

Fellow Olympian Michael Phelps has been open about his ADHD growing up. "I had a teacher tell me . . . I would never be successful," he said in 2017. As the best swimmer in history, he proved that teacher wrong!

Leonardo da Vinci

Brittney Spears

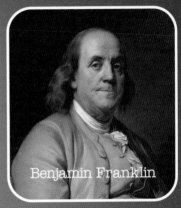

Benjamin Franklin

THE FACES OF ADHD

Lots of people throughout history have been diagnosed with ADHD. Others showed symptoms before anyone knew what ADHD was.

- Leonardo da Vinci
- Brittney Spears
- Will Smith
- Will.i.am
- Zooey Deschanel
- Ryan Gosling

- Justin Timberlake
- Solange Knowles
- Wolfgang Amadeus Mozart
- John F. Kennedy
- Benjamin Franklin
- Alexander Graham Bell

GOING FOR GOLD

When I was first diagnosed with ADHD, I was afraid I wouldn't amount to anything. I really love to swim, and I dream of one day swimming in the Olympics.

My counselor told me some of the most successful people in the world have ADHD. He said one of my heroes, Michael Phelps, has it. I found out he stayed focused by competing in swimming, which helped him organize his time. When he struggled, his mom helped him. He ended up winning 23 Olympic gold medals!

My dad's also always there for me. He drives me to practice and reminds me of important races. I'm so lucky to have his help. He believes I'll go to the Olympics one day . . . So do I!

People with ADHD can succeed in life just like anyone else, with extra focus on good habits.

Chapter 2

UNDERSTANDING ADHD

Lots of people have one or many symptoms of ADHD. Some symptoms are also common with other conditions. To decide if someone has ADHD, doctors use standards set by the American Psychiatric Association. The association has lists of several symptoms for both types of ADHD.

Many types of doctors, such as psychiatrists and **psychologists**, can diagnose ADHD.

Children up to 16 years old must have at least six symptoms for at least six months to be diagnosed. People 17 years and older must have at least five. Symptoms may be different for adults.

OTHER CONSIDERATIONS

In addition to the symptoms, other conditions must be met for a diagnosis. They include:

- Several symptoms must be seen before age 12.

- Symptoms must happen in two or more places, such as at home, work, or school.

- Symptoms must get in the way of life.

- Symptoms can't be explained by other conditions.

Find Out More

For a full list of all symptoms, visit *cdc.gov/ncbddd/adhd/diagnosis.html*. However, only an official doctor can give a diagnosis.

ADHD IN GIRLS AND WOMEN

For a long time, people believed that only boys could have ADHD. This is because girls and women sometimes show different symptoms. Girls and women also tend to hide, or mask, their symptoms.

Girls with ADHD are often misdiagnosed as having **anxiety** or **depression**.

Since some doctors only consider symptoms common to boys, girls can go underdiagnosed. Both boys and girls can have any or all of the symptoms of ADHD. Boys, however, are more likely to have the hyperactive type of ADHD. Girls are more likely to have the inattentive type.

Fast Fact

More than twice as many boys aged three to 17 are diagnosed with ADHD as girls.

ADHD SYMPTOMS COMMON IN GIRLS

- Talking a lot
- Easily making friends but can't keep them
- Staying in unhealthy relationships
- Masking symptoms
- Having low self-worth, anxiety, or depression
- Being more likely to self-harm, become pregnant, or smoke at an early age

NOT JUST A SILLY GIRL

For as long as I can remember, I've struggled at school and home. My teachers got on me for talking in class. They said I daydreamed too much. My parents told me I needed to get serious and punished me for bad grades.

It made me feel bad about myself. I started hiding my **impulses** to talk to friends. I worked even harder than my classmates just to keep my grades up. I didn't want people to think I was a silly girl who wasn't good at school.

I became so anxious I started vaping. My parents sent me to a counselor when they realized how much I was struggling. She said I have ADHD. She also explained my ADHD likely went undiagnosed because my symptoms are different from a boy's.

Girls with ADHD may look like they're daydreaming in class, but really their minds are racing.

WHAT'S TO BLAME?

Doctors aren't entirely sure what causes ADHD. They believe **genetics** may play a part. That means you're more likely to have ADHD if one or both of your parents have it.

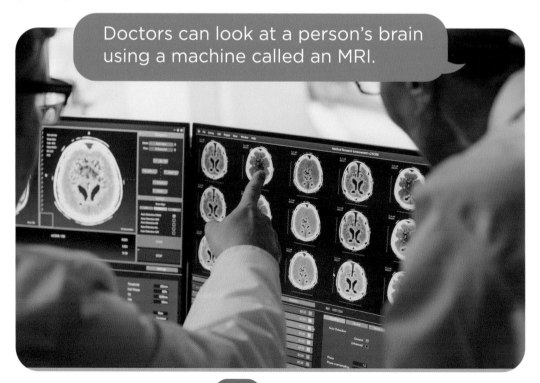

Doctors can look at a person's brain using a machine called an MRI.

Scientists are trying to figure out what may be behind the condition. Knowing possible causes could help doctors come up with new treatments. Common misunderstandings are that eating too much sugar or watching too much TV cause ADHD. Health studies show there's little support for these ideas.

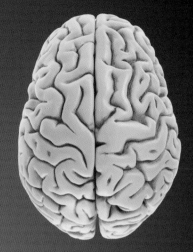

Fast Fact

Some studies show certain areas of the brain may be smaller or bigger for people with ADHD.

COULD THESE CAUSE ADHD?

Scientists are studying these possible causes of ADHD:

- Brain injury, or harm
- Contact with unsafe matter in one's surroundings
- **Alcohol** and/or **tobacco** use during a mother's pregnancy
- Early birth
- Low weight at birth

COEXISTING CONDITIONS

ADHD symptoms can mask, or hide, other conditions. More than two-thirds of people with ADHD have at least one other condition. These are called coexisting conditions. This is why it's so important to see a doctor for a diagnosis. Coexisting conditions may change how ADHD is treated.

Up to half of parents of children with ADHD say their child has trouble sleeping.

CONDITIONS THAT COMMONLY OVERLAP WITH ADHD

- **Oppositional Defiant Disorder**
  - o Arguing with others
  - o Not following rules
  - o Anger

- **Conduct Disorder**
  - o Forceful behavior
  - o Lying
  - o Stealing

- **Mood Disorders**
  - o Depression
  - o Mania
  - o Bipolar disorder (mania and depression)

- **Anxiety**
  - o Deep worry
  - o Tiredness

- **Tics and Tourette's Syndrome**
  - o Tics are fast, uncontrolled movements
  - o Tourette's syndrome involves flinching, or drawing away, and repeated yelling or making sounds

- **Learning Disorders**
  - o Trouble reading called dyslexia
  - o Trouble with math called dyscalculia
  - o Speech problems

- **Substance Abuse**
  - o Early tobacco use
  - o Misuse of alcohol
  - o Drug abuse

- **Sleep disorders**
  - o Trouble falling or staying asleep

Chapter 3

GETTING HELP

There's no cure for ADHD yet. But there are many ways to treat it. Treatment for ADHD depends on a person's symptoms, personality, and family life.

The two main types of treatment are behavior **therapy** and medication, or drugs. People with ADHD may receive either—or both. For young people with ADHD, their parents may also receive therapy or training to help their child.

These treatments can help people with ADHD live a happier life. They can also improve a person's connections with other people.

Sometimes treatments will include eating healthier foods.

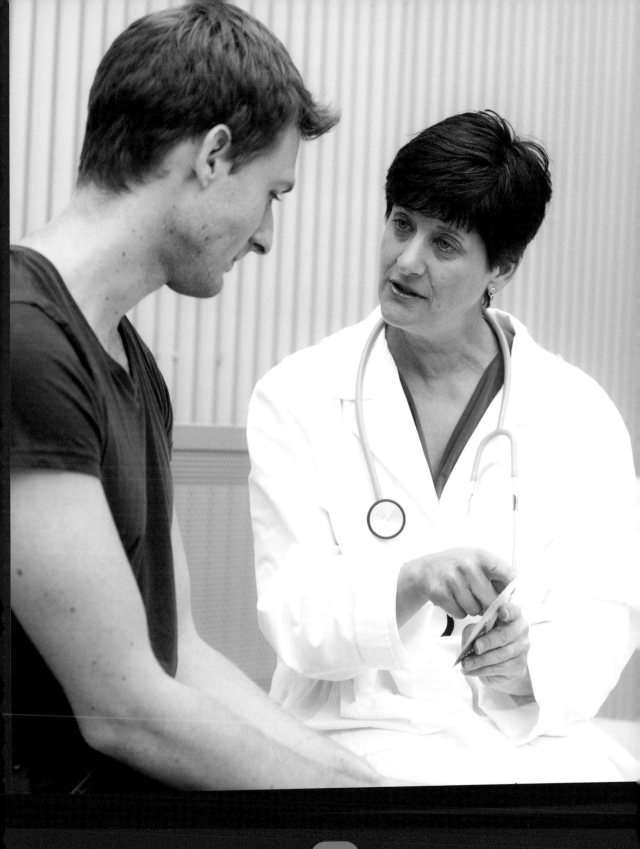

BEHAVIOR THERAPY

Therapy is one of the best ways to control ADHD symptoms. One study showed that children deal with the condition better if they receive therapy before trying medication. Many people end up using both therapy and medication, and that's OK!

ADHD can lead to secondary conditions, such as depression and anxiety. Therapy can help with those.

WAYS BEHAVIOR THERAPY CAN HELP

- Pay better attention during school
- Learn positive behaviors at home
- Ease outbursts
- Learn tips to stay organized
- Complete homework and other tasks on time

What Is CBT?

Some people with ADHD may also benefit from **cognitive** behavioral therapy (CBT). This type of treatment helps people to change their thinking patterns. It's also helpful for people who have depression from dealing with ADHD.

HAVE FUN!

Some forms of therapy can be helpful and fun. Do you think one of these might help?

- Music therapy: Helps focus attention, ease hyperactivity, and strengthen social skills
- Art therapy: Helps with sharing thoughts using pictures, and directing energy and focus on art projects
- Equine, or horse, therapy: Teaches how to read bodily cues

ANOTHER OPTION

Doctors may order medicine for their ADHD patients. There are many kinds of ADHD drugs that treat different symptoms. Most fall into one of three types.

SOME WELL-KNOWN ADHD DRUGS

Stimulants: Drugs that can work quickly. They increase matter in the brain to improve attention and compel action.

o Adderall
o Ritalin
o Dexedrine
o Concerta
o Vyvanse

Nonstimulants: Drugs that often work slower. They increase matter in the brain to improve focus and control impulses.

o Strattera
o Intuniv
o Tenex
o Qelbree
o Kapvay

Antidepressants: A drug used to lessen a person's feelings of depression.
- o Wellbutrin
- o Norpramin
- o Tofranil
- o Aventyl
- o Pamelor

Side Effects

ADHD medicines can also cause side effects. These can include sleepiness, dizziness, dry mouth, and upset stomach. People on these drugs may also lose weight, stop eating, and sleep less. It's important to tell a parent and doctor if you have bad side effects.

Most ADHD medications are only available as prescriptions. This means a doctor must order the medicine through a pharmacy, or drugstore.

HELP AT SCHOOL

ADHD can be extra difficult to deal with at school. Teachers expect students to pay attention and sit still in class. Some students with ADHD struggle with both.

The law requires that all students be able to get an education no matter their health conditions. Luckily, students, parents, and teachers can set up a plan for success! This may include allowing extra time to take tests and quizzes. Students might also take special education classes or even get breaks to move around and burn some energy.

Some plans may suggest students use special technology to help with schoolwork. Technology is a method that uses science to solve problems, as well as the tools used to solve those problems. Tools can include computers, tablets, and more.

MAKING A PLAN

Students can receive help through an Individualized Education Program (IEP) or through a 504 Plan. Both are supported by laws that keep students with disabilities safe. You can ask a doctor, teacher, counselor, and a parent which is right for you.

● IEP Plan
Who: Children who have one or more of 13 types of disabilities (ADHD is one)
Where: All public schools

● 504 Plan
Who: Children with diagnosed physical or mental disabilities that seriously limit learning
Where: All public schools

SUPPORTING EACH OTHER

My best friend at school, Zach, was recently diagnosed with ADHD—just like me! I've been giving him lots of advice on how to deal with the different symptoms. We're so lucky to have each other for support.

But Zach's still struggling to keep his grades up. Reading homework is hard for him because he also has dyslexia. He also needs extra help remembering due dates. I told him he should talk to his dad about an IEP plan, like I have.

They had a meeting at school and came up with ways to help Zach. Now our English teacher gives him shorter reading homework. He also gets extra time in school to finish tests with a lot of reading. He's even got a big new binder that holds folders for his classes. I think we'll both be OK!

Friends and family can help people with ADHD handle their symptoms.

LOOKING FORWARD

For many children, the symptoms of ADHD decrease as they get older. That's why some people think of it as a childhood condition. But many adults have ADHD. In fact, some people aren't diagnosed with ADHD until they are adults, and their symptoms aren't as clear as in childhood.

Adults with ADHD can improve their brain's executive function. Some tips include completing work step-by-step and using pictures to help with organization.

Like children, adults with ADHD have trouble paying attention. They can also be impulsive and anxious. Daily tasks, such as cleaning and taking care of bills, can be hard.

Fast Fact

About 10 million adults have ADHD.

EXECUTIVE FUNCTION

Executive function is the brain's ability to get things done. This can be hard for adults with ADHD, causing trouble at work and school. Executive function allows people to:

- Use time wisely
- Organize work
- Work on multiple things at once
- Remember information
- Work independently

FACING STIGMA

Like many diseases and mental health conditions, ADHD unfairly has a stigma. That means that some people have negative, or harmful, opinions about the condition. Even people who have ADHD may feel negatively about it.

The stigma that comes with ADHD can make it even harder to deal with.

In some cases, people may not believe ADHD is even real. They may think the person is just being lazy or acting badly. Some people think children are overmedicated for the condition. Teachers may also think a person is just a bad student.

Talking Points

Here are some ways to respond if someone is being negative about your ADHD:

Negative statement: "You just need to stop being lazy."
Response: "I have ADHD. It's just as real as any other health condition."

Negative statement: "You need to calm down and sit still."
Response: "I know I can be squirmy. I have ADHD and am working to control my impulses."

Negative statement: "You're too young to use medication."
Response: "ADHD medication helps my mind focus on school and work. My doctor is keeping an eye on me."

THE NEXT STEP

Have you read this book and thought, "This sounds like me?" You might have ADHD. But there's only one way to know for sure. You must get a diagnosis from a trained doctor. Many other conditions share the same symptoms and could be mistaken for ADHD.

Talk to your parents, guardians, school counselor, or doctor about being tested. You may have to visit a special doctor, such as a psychiatrist or therapist, who can do the testing.

Children and Adults with Attention-Deficit/Hyperactivity Disorder (CHADD)

www.chadd.org
4221 Forbes Blvd. Suite 270
Lanham, MD 20706
(301) 306-7070
CHADD offers information about ADHD symptoms, treatment, and even money for college. The website also includes a list of counselors, psychiatrists, and other doctors who can help.

Centers for Disease Control and Prevention (CDC)

www.cdc.gov/ncbddd/adhd/index.html
1600 Clifton Road
Atlanta, GA 30329
(800) 232-4636

The CDC website has facts and figures, treatment suggestions, and studies related to ADHD. You can also learn about laws protecting people with the condition.

ADHD organizations and support groups offer lots of information online. Try doing some more reading, and talk to your doctor!

Feeling Positive

Even though I was scared when I learned I had ADHD, I'm glad I have a diagnosis. It means I now have answers about my struggles.

I often meet with my therapist to talk about my feelings. I take medicine every day, so my symptoms aren't as bad. I have an IEP so teachers let me have more time on tests. They also help me stay organized. My school counselor has also helped me find ways to improve my grades.

I get along better with my family and friends. Now that my parents know why my grades were suffering, we have fewer fights. My friends understand why I sometimes can't focus during chats.

I still struggle a little, but I'm sure I now have the tools to succeed!

Skills teens learn to cope with ADHD can be used as they deal the condition into adulthood.

GLOSSARY

alcohol: A clear liquid that has a strong smell and can make a
person drunk.

anxiety: Fear or nervousness about what might happen.
Anxious means experiencing unease and nervousness,
often about something that hasn't happened yet.

ashamed: Feeling shame or blame.

association: An organized group of people who have the
same interests.

behave: To act in a proper manner.

behavior: The way a person acts. Behavioral means relating to
the way someone acts or behaves.

cognitive: Dealing with the mind, such as thinking and understanding.

counselor: A person whose job is to talk with people about
their emotions and help them make decisions.

depression: A feeling of sadness. Also, a serious medical condition
in which someone's feelings of sadness and hopelessness
cause problems in their everyday life.

genetics: The science that studies genes, which is information
inherited, or gained from, two parents that decides
how a person looks and acts.

impulse: A sudden stirring up of the mind and spirit to do something.

mania: Mental illness in which a person becomes extra excited, active, or emotional.

physical: Relating to the body of a person.

psychiatric: Relating to the branch of medicine that involves mental, emotional, and behavioral health conditions. A psychiatrist is a medical doctor who focuses on mental health.

psychologist: A doctor who deals with the mind or behavior. They cannot prescribe medication like a psychiatrist can.

severe: Bad, serious, or unpleasant. Severity is how bad or serious something is.

substance: A drug that is considered harmful.

therapy: The treatment of physical or mental illness.

tobacco: A plant and leaves that are smoked in cigarettes and pipes.

treatment: Medical care for an illness or injury.

INDEX